Welcome to Vocabulary Power

damp

Something that is damp is slightly moist or wet.

Make it fun!

- Read a word every day with your child. Make it a special time that you both look forward to. At breakfast or before bed, a few minutes a day will make a lifetime of difference in your child's education.

- Look at the illustration. How does it show the meaning of the word? Ask your child to brainstorm another way to express the same idea in a picture.

- Read the question at the bottom of the page. Can you or your child guess the answer? Use the word in a question, sentence, or riddle of your own.

- Encourage your child to use each new word at least three times during the next day.

Context Is Everything

- Literacy experts agree that developing early vocabulary is the key to future learning. A deficiency in vocabulary as early as third grade can prove virtually insurmountable in later life.

- Research shows that children with a strong vocabulary do better in school and move joyfully along the road to academic success.

- A child with a strong vocabulary is not only a better reader, but also benefits from greater self-esteem. Confident kids are happy kids!

Where These 200 Words Come From

Kids love learning the meaning of words that they encounter in their favorite books. We compiled our 200 words from the world's most popular and beloved children's literature. Educators regard our word collection as a key component for developing a child's vocabulary.

The Team

AUTHOR, Audrey Carangelo has twenty years' experience developing language arts, reading, and phonics curricula used in classrooms nationwide. She has written dozens of books for beginning readers.

SPECIAL THANKS to the wonderful involvement of Catherine Rupf, Anne Burrus, Frédéric Michaud, Audrey Carangelo, Adrienne Schure, Joe and Denise Kiernan, and the great team of the Bill SMITH STUDIO.

TimeLine™

TimeLine
EXPLORERS
From Egypt to Mars

HISTORY UNFOLDS   More Brain Power

TimeLine
INVENTIONS
From Rocks to Rockets

HISTORY UNFOLDS   More Brain Power

TimeLine
PRESIDENTS
From Independence to Now

HISTORY UNFOLDS   More Brain Power

Pronunciation Guide

Vowels

a	cat	ow	cow, mouth
ah	father, car, pot	u	cook, put
ay	say, tame, paid, pair, scare	uh	fun, action, soda, about, trouble, travel
aw	law, caught	ur	curve, nerve, better
e	bet, send	yoo	mule
ee	meet, seat, ear		
i	fit		
ie	pie, bite, eye, sigh		
oh	so, slow, bone		
oo	school, pool		
or	born, score		
oi	boil, coin, boy		

Consonants

b	book, bear	p	pen, sip
ch	match, chop	r	ribbon, car
d	dog, bed	s	sat, rice, class
f	fit, cliff, phone	sh	shape, rush
g	got, bag	t	tell, bat
h	how, whole	th	thin, both
j	jar, germ, badge	*th*	the, breathe
k	cat, quit, keep, sock	v	vine, save
l	let, tall	w	will, white
m	mad, lamb	y	you
n	no, ten, know	z	zap
ng	song	zh	treasure

Available in the Series

Whistle

(**WIS** – uhl) *verb*

Tweet

When you whistle, you make a sound by putting your lips together and blowing air through them.

? Why can't chickens whistle?

! They don't have any lips!

Creature

(**KREE** - chur) *noun*

A creature is a living being, like a human or animal.

? Which of these is *not* a creature: a caterpillar, a girl, a tree or a fish?

! Only the tree is not a creature.

Annoy

(uh – **NOI**) *verb*

When you annoy someone, you bother him or her.

? Which might annoy you: someone poking you, or someone asking you for directions?

! Someone poking you would annoy you!

Empty

(**EMP** – tee) *adjective*

If a container is empty, it doesn't have anything inside of it.

? What can be half empty and half full at the same time?

! Half a glass of water.

Obedient

(oh – **BEE** – dee – uhnt) *adjective*

3

People and animals that
are obedient do what
they are told to do.

What an
obedient
dog!

? Your dad tells you to make the bed and
you do. Are you obedient? Yes, or no?

! Yes, you are obedient. Good for you!

Foam

(FOHM) *noun*

Foam is a layer of tiny, sudsy bubbles.

? How is root beer like a bubble bath?

❶ Both make foam. But don't take a bath in root beer!

Amphibian

(am – **FIB** – ee – uhn) *noun*

An amphibian is an animal that lives on the land and in the water. Frogs are amphibians.

? At an amphibian birthday party, do they play in the pool, or in the yard?

! Both!

Courage

(**KUR** – ij) *noun*

If you have courage, you are brave and fearless.

❓ What kind of lion has no courage?

❗ A dandelion!

Whammy

(**WAM** – ee) *noun*

A whammy is when something unexpected and unpleasant happens.

? Would you call a surprise spelling test a whammy?

! Yes. A surprise test is unexpected.

Halt

(HAWLT) *verb*

To halt means to stop.

? Why did the chicken halt
before crossing the road?

! Because he saw a stop sign.

Embarrass

(em – **BA** – ruhs) *verb*

When you embarrass
someone, you make that person
feel bad and uncomfortable.

? Which might embarrass you: someone laughing at you for
making a mistake, or making a mistake when you are alone?

! When someone laughs at you for making a mistake, it
might embarrass you!

Damp

(DAMP) *adjective*

Something that is damp is slightly moist or wet.

? What did the mold say when he entered the damp basement?

! Honey, I'm home!

Crunch

(KRUHNCH) *verb*

Things that crunch make a crisp noise when you bite, step on or smash them.

Crunch!

? **What will crunch in winter when you step on it?**

! **Snow!**

Icicle

(**IE** – si – kuhl) *noun*

An icicle is a long, pointed piece of ice.

❓ During which season would you find icicles: summer, or winter?

❗ You'd find icicles in the winter, not the summer!

Humble

(**HUHM** – buhl) *adjective*

A humble person does not brag about herself.

I'd like to thank my teammates.

You are so humble!

? **Do humble people tell everyone how smart they are?**

! **No. If you're humble, you don't brag.**

Absent

(**AB** – suhnt) *adjective*

Sally is absent today!

A person who is absent is not present.

? If someone is absent from school, are they in class?

! No. If the person is absent from school, the person is not there.

Scorn
(**SKORN**) *verb*

If you scorn someone or something, you look down on them and treat them badly.

? Is it fair to scorn someone just because they look different from you?

! No. To scorn others because of their looks is not right.

Enthusiasm

(en – **THOO** – zee – az – uhm) *noun*

He has such enthusiasm!

Enthusiasm is great interest in, or excitement about, something.

? **What's the best way to do your school work?**

Zone

(ZOHN) *noun*

Always cross in the crossing zone!

A zone is an area with a special purpose. Your school might have a quiet zone.

? Is it safe to be in a danger zone?

! No. Stay away from danger zones!

Conquer

(**KAHN** – kur) *verb*

To conquer is to take control of people or things. You can conquer your enemies or your fears.

YOU WIN!

? If one group of ants conquer another group's hill, do they take it over?

! Yes. The hill is now theirs.

Bitter

(**BIT** – ur) *adjective*

A bitter taste is strong and unpleasant.

? What did the robin say when he ate the bitter worm?

❗ Yuck! I wish I hadn't been such an early bird!

Canoe

(kuh – **NOO**) *noun*

A canoe is a narrow boat that you paddle.

? How is using a canoe like playing ping-pong?

! You need a paddle for both.

Festive

(**FES** – tiv) *adjective*

Something that is festive is colorful and fun. Holidays and other celebrations are festive.

? What did the chicken say to the peacock?

! You look festive!

(KOHD) *noun*

A **code** is a secret way to send information using words, numbers and pictures.

? What did one bird say in code to another as they were eating worms?

Paradise

(**PA** – ruh – dies) *noun*

A place that you think is very beautiful and happy can be called paradise.

? Can a mud puddle be a paradise?

! Sure, if you're a pig!

Education

(ed – juh – **KAY** – shuhn) *noun*

Education is the knowledge, skills and abilities gained from going to school.

SCHOOLHOUSE

? Is math part of your education?

! Yes. Math is a very important subject.

Shadow

(SHAD - oh) *noun*

When an object stands in front of a light, it makes a shadow on the ground, floor or wall.

? If a cat sees his shadow on a sidewalk, is it a sunny day, or a dark night?

! The cat sees his shadow on a sunny day.

Magnet

(**MAG** – nit) *noun*

A magnet is a piece of metal that attracts iron or steel.

? What did the nail say to the magnet?

! I'm very attracted to you!

Whiskers

(**WISK** – urs) *noun*

An animal's whiskers are the long, stiff hairs by its mouth. A man's beard can also be called whiskers.

? Why do cats have whiskers?

! So they have something to shave in the morning!

Benefit

(**BEN** – uh – fit) *verb*

We benefit from this tree!

If you benefit from something, you are helped by it.

? How can you benefit from a fruit tree?

! It gives you good food to eat and shade, too.

Rumble

(**RUHM** – buhl) *noun*

rumble rumble

A rumble is a low, steady noise.

? How is a train like your tummy?

! They can both rumble.

Peril

(**PER** – uhl) *noun*

If you are in peril, it means you are in danger.

? What did the lobster say when he was in peril?

! I'm in hot water now!

Flicker

(**FLIK** – ur) *verb*

A light or flame that flickers shines unsteadily.

? If a candle's flame flickers, what might happen next?

! When a flame flickers, it might go out!

Encourage

(en - **KUR** - ij) *verb*

Come on, you can do it!

To encourage means to give help and support to someone so they can do their best.

? What are some things you can say to encourage a friend?

! Way to go! Keep it up! You're doing great!

Howl

(HOWL) *noun, verb*

HOOOOW!

A howl is a long cry made by an animal. Wolves and dogs howl.

? Why do wolves howl at the moon?

! Because they can't quack!

Calm

(**KAHM**) *adjective*

Stay calm, I'll fix it!

If someone is calm, that person is peaceful and quiet.

? Is an angry person calm?

! No. An angry person is not peaceful at all.

Silent

(**SIE** – luhnt) *adjective*

To be silent is to be completely quiet.

? When are tomatoes silent?

! When they're reading books in the library!

Pebble

(**PEB** – uhl) *noun*

A pebble is small, round stone.

? What's a pebble's favorite chair?

! A rocker!

Climate

(KLIE – muht) *noun*

The weather conditions of a particular place are called its climate.

I love this cold climate!

? Is the climate of the North Pole warm and dry?

! No. The North Pole is very cold and snowy!

Frazzled

(**FRAZ** - uhld) *adjective*

If you are frazzled, you are tired in mind and body.

My kids have me frazzled!

? Can doing too many things at once make you frazzled?

! Yes. Too much work can make you feel tired all over.

Cherish

(**CHER** – ish) *verb*

To cherish is to care for a person or thing very much.

 Can you cherish a friend?

❗ Yes. You cherish people you care about.

Adjust

(uh – **JUHST**) *verb*

How do you like the coat?

I can adjust it!

When you adjust something, you change it so that it pleases you.

? Can you adjust a belt to be smaller or larger?

! Yes. You can make it fit just right.

Fortunate

(**FOR** – chuh – nuht) *adjective*

Someone who is fortunate is lucky.

? What do you call a fortunate bird who lives on water?

! A lucky ducky!

Caper

(**KAY** - pur) *noun*

A caper is a trick or a prank.
Caper is also another word
for a crime.

? Which animal looks like he's ready
for a caper?

! A raccoon — he's always wearing
a mask!

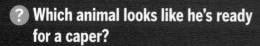

Million

(**MIL** – yuhn) *noun*

A million is a very large number.
A million is written 1,000,000.

That must
be a
million
years old!

? Which is closer to a million: the number
of stars in the night sky, or the number of
houses on your street?

! There are millions of stars in the sky!

Rescue

(**RES** – kyoo) *verb*

If you rescue someone or something, you save them from danger.

? Which dog is known to rescue people trapped in the snow?

! A Saint Bernard.

Slim

(**SLIM**) *adjective*

I'm sooooo slim!

A slim animal, person or thing is thin and not heavy.

? Which is slim: a snake, or a hippo?

! Snakes are very thin.

Patient

(**PAY** – shuhnt) *noun*

I'm sorry you had to wait.
You are a very patient patient!

A patient is someone who is
receiving medical treatment
from a doctor.

❓ Why do cats make such
good patients?

❗ They always behave
"purrrrfectly"!

Allowance

(uh – **LOW** – uhns) *noun*

An **allowance** is money that is given to someone on a regular basis.

Can I have my allowance, please?

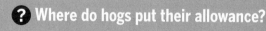

? Where do hogs put their allowance?

! In the piggy bank!

Amiss

(uh – **MIS**) *adjective*

Something is amiss in my garden!

When you say that something is amiss, it means that something is wrong or out of place.

? If all the flowers in your garden are gone, is something amiss?

! Yes. Something is wrong.

Flatter

(**FLAT** – ur) *verb*

When you flatter people, you say nice things to them, usually to get them to do something for you.

You are so handsome! I know you'll let me go.

? How did the wolf flatter the chickens?

! You are so beautiful! Won't you let me take you out for a bite?

Coward

(**KOW** - urd) *noun*

Come here, you coward!

A coward is someone who is easily scared, and runs away from frightening situations.

? Why is a hen a coward?

! Because it's always chicken.

Poem

(**POHM**) noun

A poem is a kind of writing with words picked for their sound and feeling. Some poems rhyme.

Roses are red
violets are blue

? What is a skunks favorite poem?

! Roses are red, violets are blue.
I'm pretty stinky. How about you?

Screech

(**SKREECH**) *verb*

SCREECH
SCREECH

SCREECH
SCREECH

When birds or other animals screech, they make a loud, high noise.

? Which would screech: a dog, or a seagull?

! Seagulls screech. Dogs bark!

Terrify

(**TER** – uh – fie) *verb*

To terrify something or someone is to scare them a lot.

❓ What might terrify you: a bunny, or a tiger chasing you?

❗ A tiger chasing you, of course!

Magazine

(mag – uh – **ZEEN**) *noun*

A magazine contains news, pictures and articles. A magazine comes out regularly and is different every time.

? What magazine do birds read?

! Newsbeak.

Ability

(uh – **BIL** – i – tee) *noun*

I have
the ability
to fly planes!

Ability is the power
to do something.

? Why would a penguin lose the ability to swim?

! He got cold feet!

Boil

(BOIL) *verb*

When you **boil** a liquid, you heat it up until it bubbles.

? What time is it when water starts to boil?

! Tea time!

Display
(dis – **PLAY**) verb

When you display something, you put it in a special place so people can see it.

? Where did the turtle display his first-prize ribbon?

! On his "shell-f"!

Castle

(**KAS** – uhl) *noun*

A **castle** is a large, stone building from a long time ago. Castles were built to keep people safe inside them.

? What kind of castle can you build with your own hands?

! A sand castle!

Astonish

(uh – **STAHN** – ish) *verb*

To astonish someone is to surprise them very much.

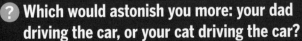

❓ Which would astonish you more: your dad driving the car, or your cat driving the car?

❗ Your cat driving the car would astonish you!

Savage

(**SAV** – uhj) *adjective*

ROAR!

Something that is savage is not tamed or under human control.

? What do you call a wild, untamed vegetable?

! A savage cabbage!

Error

(**ER** – ur) *noun*

I think there is an error!

An error is a mistake.

? What's one way to apologize if you make an error?

! Oops! My mistake. I'm sorry.

Fountain

(**FOWN** – tuhn) *noun*

A **fountain** is a stream of water used for drinking or decoration.

? How can you tell if a fountain is popular?

! It makes a big splash!

Jumble

(**JUHM** – buhl) *noun*

**What a jumble!
I can't find my shoe!**

A **jumble** is a mix of different things in a messy pile.

? If your toys are in a messy pile, are they in a jumble?

! Yes. Time to clean up!

Advice

(ad - **VIES**) *noun*

> My advice is that you study!

Test Tomorrow!

Advice is a suggestion offered as help to someone making a decision.

? What advice did the dog give to the shy porcupine?

! You need to stick up for yourself!

Stumble

(**STUHM** – buhl) *verb*

To stumble means to trip or lose your balance while walking or running.

? What did the snail say when he started to stumble?

! Oops! I better slow down!

Cautious

(**KAW** – shuhs) *adjective*

Don't worry.
I'm very cautious!

If you are cautious, you are careful
to avoid mistakes and danger.

? How did the chicken cross the road?

! He was very cautious, and looked both ways.

Banner

(**BAN** - ur) *noun*

A banner is a strip of material with writing and pictures that is carried or hung.

Go Bears

When would you carry a banner: in a supermarket, or in a parade?

In a parade!

Eager

(**EE** – gur) *adjective*

If you are eager to do something, you want to do it very much.

I'm eager for the ride to start!

ROLLERCOASTER

❓ Which animal wants very much to build a dam?

❗ An eager beaver.

Creak

(KREEK) *noun, verb*

A **creak** is a short, squeaky sound. Chairs and doors may **creak** when they move.

creak creak

? When the door made a creak, what did it say to the oil can?

! Come here, you little squirt!

Experience

(eks – **PEER** – ee – uhns) *noun*

What an experience!

An experience is something that a person has done or lived through.

❓ Which sounds like a more exciting experience: riding in a hot air balloon, or taking a nap?

❗ Riding in a hot air balloon would be a very exciting experience.

Prevent

(pri – **VENT**) *verb*

> I want to prevent my bike from being stolen!

When you prevent something, you make sure it doesn't happen.

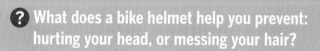

❓ What does a bike helmet help you prevent: hurting your head, or messing your hair?

❗ A helmet keeps your head safe!

Slither

(**SLITH** – ur) *verb*

**Something that slithers slides
along like a snake.**

? Why did the snake slither
through the park?

! He left his jogging shoes
at home!

Tremendous

(truh – **MEN** – duhs) *adjective*

Something or someone tremendous is very strong or large.

What a tremendous wave!

? **Which has tremendous winds: a breeze, or a tornado?**

! A tornado has tremendous winds!

(FRAY grunht) *adjective*

These flowers are fragrant!

Something fragrant smells pleasant.

? Which would you say is more fragrant: a field of flowers, or cut grass?

! Flowers are more fragrant.

Coarse

(KORS) *adjective*

This sweater is too coarse!

If something is coarse, it feels very rough and scratchy.

? What do you call a pony with an itchy coat?

! A coarse horse!

Avoid

(uh - **VOID**) *verb*

When you avoid a person or place, you stay away from it.

? Why did the boy avoid the skunk?

! He had a lot of "scents"!

Gossip

(**GAHS** – ip) *verb, noun*

To gossip **is to talk about someone's secrets when they are not around.** Gossip **is not polite.**

? What should you do if you hear gossip?

! Don't share it with anyone. It's not nice!

(GRAD - joo - uhl) *adjective*

If something is **gradual**, it takes place slowly over time.

? Which is gradual: how a snowman melts, or how a stick breaks?

! A snowman melting is a gradual change.

Approach
(uh – **PROHCH**) verb

Number 5 is approaching the Finish Line!

When you approach something, you move closer to it.

? Should you approach a pet you don't know?

! No. Never approach an animal that you don't know.

Coral

(**KOR** – uhl) *noun*

The skeletons of thousands of tiny sea creatures make up a coral reef.

? **If you are swimming and see some coral, should you take some?**

! No. Coral is special, and should never be harmed.

Stern

(**STURN**) *adjective*

Class Rules
No Talking
No Gum Chewing
No Fighting

Someone who is stern is very strict and serious.

? Do stern people like rules?

! Yes. Stern people love rules!

Pollute

(puh – **LOOT**) *verb*

To pollute is to add things such as trash and smoke to the air, water and land that make them dirty and harmful.

? Can a factory pollute the air with dark smoke?

! Yes. A factory can pollute the air and water!

Purse
(PURS) *noun*

A purse is a small bag that can hold keys and other things.

? Why doesn't a kangaroo carry a purse?

! She keeps everything in her pouch!

Fuel

(**FYOOL**) *noun*

Fuel is a source of energy or heat. Coal, gas and oil are all types of fuel.

❓ What does the human body use for fuel?

❗ Food gives our bodies energy.

Expert

(**EKS** – purt) *noun*

I'm a butterfly expert.

An expert is a person who is skilled at doing something or knows a lot about a subject.

? What kind of expert knows a lot about clothes?

! A smarty-pants!

Breeze

(BREEZ) *noun*

A breeze is a gentle wind.

? When is a breeze like a motor?

! When it makes your sailboat go!

Hawk

(HAWK) *noun*

A hawk is a large bird with sharp claws that eats small animals.

? What did one hawk say to the other?

! Who are you having for lunch?

Snarl
(**SNAHRL**) *verb*

To snarl is to show your teeth and growl fiercely.

❓ If you see an animal snarl, is it happy?

❗ Probably not. Stay away!

Cheap

(CHEEP) *noun*

This is so cheap!

Things that have a low price are called cheap.

? Which would you call cheap: a bike that costs ten dollars, or an ice cream cone that costs ten dollars?

! A bike that costs ten dollars. A ten-dollar ice cream cone is expensive!

Acquaintance

(uh – **KWAY** – tuhns) *noun*

He's an acquaintance from school!

An acquaintance **is someone you know, but who is not a close friend.**

? Which is an acquaintance: your best friend, or someone you know from gym class?

! Someone from gym class is an acquaintance. Your best friend is much more!

Seize

(SEEZ) *verb*

When you seize something or someone, you take hold of them quickly and strongly.

? Who would seize a crook?

! A policeman would seize a crook.

I seized the crook!

47

Envy
(**EN** – vee) *verb*

I envy you!
I want a
pogo stick too!

To envy is to want something
another person has.

? What happened when the frog
wanted his friend's lily pad?

! He became green with envy.

Beast

(**BEEST**) *noun*

I'm king of the beasts!

A beast is a wild, dangerous animal.

? What is it called when a group of lions have dinner together?

! A beast feast!

Delight

(di – **LIET**) *verb*

If something delights you,
it pleases you very much.

? Are flowers the only way to delight
a friend?

! No. A kind word does the trick too!

Blot

(BLAHT) *noun*

A blot is a drop of spilled liquid, like ink or paint.

? Which might leave a blot: water, or blue paint?

! Blue paint would make a messy blot.

Scurry

(**SKUR** – ee) *verb*

People or animals that scurry move quickly because they are frightened.

? Why did the mice scurry across the floor?

! You'd scurry too, if you were someone's lunch!

Harm

(**HAHRM**) *verb*

Sorry, I meant no harm!

To harm someone is to hurt them in some way.

? **Can friends harm each other?**

! **Yes, but they always say they're sorry.**

Cheat

(**CHEET**) *verb*

If you cheat, you act dishonestly to get what you want.

? **What happened to the bar of soap that decided to cheat on the test?**

! **They caught him and he was all washed up!**

Ooze

(**OOZ**) verb

When a thick liquid oozes,
it flows slowly.

? **What might ooze: honey from a hive, or water from a glass?**

! **Honey will ooze from a hive. Water pours from a glass.**

Improve

(im - **PROOV**) *verb*

Nice job! You've improved your spelling!

If you improve, you get better or make something better.

? What can you do to improve your grades?

! Study, study, study!

150

Task

(TASK) *noun*

A **task** is one piece of work you have to do.

Your **task** for the day is to write about your family.

? What **task** do squirrels do before winter?

! They gather nuts.

Slender

(**SLEN** - dur) *adjective*

Someone or something slender is thin or slim.

? Which vegetable is always slender?

! A string bean.

Appreciate

(uh – **PREE** – shee – ayt) *verb*

If you appreciate what someone has done for you, you are thankful for it.

I appreciate your kindness!

? What might your dog appreciate?

! A fun game of catch!

Confuse

(kuhn – **FYOOZ**) *verb*

If something confuses you, you don't know what to do.

I'm confused. Which way should I go?

❓ Which might confuse you: directions to a birthday party, or directions for opening a door?

❗ Directions to someone's house can sometimes confuse you.

Imitate

(**IM** – uh – tayt) *verb*

When you imitate someone, you copy what they do.

? **What animal always imitates others?**

❗ A copycat!

Acorn

(**AY** – korn) *noun*

**An acorn is the seed
of an oak tree.**

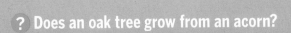

? Does an oak tree grow from an acorn?

! Yes. A big oak grows from a tiny acorn.

Opportunity

(ahp – ur – **TOO** – nuh – tee) *noun*

An opportunity is a chance for you to do something that you want to do.

? Why do snakes like to shed their skin?

! It gives them the opportunity to wear something new!

Squeeze

(SKWEEZ) *verb*

When you **squeeze** something,
you press hard on it from all sides.

? What did the toothbrush say to
the toothpaste?

! You're my main squeeze!

Villain

(**VIL** – uhn) *noun*

A **villain** is someone who hurts others or breaks the law.

❓ In the story of Little Red Riding Hood, who is the villain?

❗ The wolf!

Lava

(**LAH** – vuh) *noun*

Lava **is the hot liquid that pours out of a volcano when it erupts.**

? How is lava like a river?

! Both are liquid and both flow.

Conversation

(kahn – vur – **SAY** – shuhn) *noun*

When people talk to each other, they are having a conversation.

? Is it polite to interrupt a conversation?

! No. You should always wait your turn to speak!

Property

(**PRAHP** – ur – tee) *noun*

Property is something that is owned by a person, such as a house, a car or land.

Get off my property!

? If you own a bicycle, is it your property?

! Yes. But it's always nice to share.

Elect

(i – **LEKT**) *verb*

Elect me for Class President!

When you elect someone, you choose the person by voting.

? Why did the animals elect the lion president?

! Because he was already a good king of the jungle!

Increase

(in – **KREES**) *verb*

To increase is to grow in size or number.

❓ What happens when you put money in your piggy bank?

❗ You increase the amount you have saved!

Scramble

(**SKRAM** – buhl) *verb*

To scramble **means to do things in a hurry.**

? If you scramble to finish your homework, do you take your time?

! No. If you scramble, you are in a rush.

Pity

(**PIT** – ee) *verb*

If you pity someone, you feel bad about that person's bad luck or suffering.

What a pity!

? If you pity someone, do you feel happy for them?

! No. To pity someone is to feel sorry for them.

Wriggle

(**RIG** – uhl) *verb*

To wriggle is to twist and turn with quick movements.

? Which might wriggle: a worm, or a shoelace?

❗ A worm. Shoelaces don't wriggle!

Gobble

(**GAHB** - uhl) *verb*

If you gobble your food, you
eat it quickly and with big bites.

? Is it polite to gobble your food?

! No. You should always take small bites
and eat slowly.

Flavor

(**FLAY** – vur) *noun*

Yum! Cherry!

The flavor of food is how it tastes. Chocolate and vanilla are flavors.

? What's your favorite ice cream flavor?

! All ice cream flavors are great!

Remind

(ruh – **MIEND**) *verb*

Don't forget your parachute!

Thanks for reminding me!

When you remind someone of something, you make the person remember it.

? If you remind someone of your birthday, do you want them to remember it?

! Yes! Everyone wants their birthday to be remembered!

Hatch

(**HACH**) *verb*

To hatch means to break out of an egg, like a baby chick.

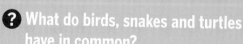

? What do birds, snakes and turtles have in common?

! They all hatch from eggs!

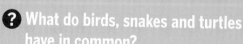

Brain

(**BRAYN**) *noun*

Your **brain** is the organ inside you skull that controls your body, thoughts, memory and feelings.

? Where is your brain located: inside your skull, or inside your shoe?

! Your brain is inside your skull. Your foot is inside your shoe!

Slab

(SLAB) *noun*

A slab is a thick, flat piece of something, such as stone or concrete.

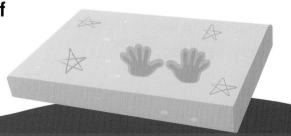

? Which can you get in a restaurant: a slab of concrete, or a slab of pie?

! A slab can also be a thick piece of pie!

Tragic

(TRAJ – ik) *adjective*

How tragic!

Something that is tragic is very, very sad.

? Which would be tragic: losing your dog, or losing your watch?

! Losing your dog would be much more tragic than losing your watch!

Wealth

(WELTH) *noun*

Wealth is a large amount of money, property or other valuables.

? Where do beavers hide their wealth?

! In the river "bank"!

Chorus

(**KOR** – uhs) *noun*

A chorus is a large group of people who sing together.

? What could you call an army chorus?

❗ A tune platoon!

Agony

(**AG** – uh – nee) *noun*

Owww! I'm in agony!

Agony is great physical or mental pain.

? Why was the carpenter in agony?

! He hit the wrong nail with his hammer!

Recognize

(**REK** – uhg – niez) *verb*

I still recognize you, Joey!

When you recognize someone, you see the person and know who the person is.

? How can you recognize a peacock?

! You recognize a peacock by its beautiful feathers.

Anxious

(**ANGK** – shuhs) *adjective*

If you are anxious, you are nervous or worried about something.

❓ If you feel anxious, do you feel relaxed?

❗ No, you feel nervous!

Expression

(ek - **SPRESH** - uhn) *noun*

Expression is a show of emotion or feeling. An expression of happiness can be a smile.

? What is a frown an expression of?

! Sadness.

Solid

(**SAHL** – id) *adjective*

Something solid is hard and firm.

? What solid was once a liquid?

 Ice!

Rustle

(**RUHS** – uhl) *verb*

I hear the leaves rustle!

Things that rustle make a soft, crackling sound as they move.

❓ Which might rustle: the pages of a newspaper, or the doorbell?

❗ Newspaper pages rustle. Doorbells ring!

Clutter

(**KLUHT** – ur) *noun*

Clutter is a messy group of things.

? Which is clutter: toys scattered around the room, or books stacked on a shelf?

! A lot of toys scattered in a room is clutter.

Absolute

(ab – suh – **LOOT**) *adjective*

Absolute means complete and total. Absolute power is complete and total power.

I am the absolute best!

World Champion

? If you have absolute control over your dog, does it listen to you?

! Yes. If you have absolute control, you are in charge.

Haul

(HAWL) *verb*

When you haul something, you move it with great effort.

? When you haul something, are you carrying something heavy?

! Yes. You haul a heavy load.

Prefer

(pri – **FUR**) *verb*

When you prefer something, you like it more than something else.

I prefer strawberry!

ICE-CREAM

? How do carrots prefer to say thank you?

! Thanks a "bunch"!

Seldom
(**SEL** – duhm) *adverb*

If something seldom happens,
it means it hardly ever happens.

? Which would you say seldom happens:
rainbows, or rain?

! Rainbows seldom happen. That's why
they are so special!

Fury

(**FYU** – ree) *noun*

Fury is violent anger or rage.

? Is someone shouting angrily and waving their fists an example of fury?

! Yes. Fury is extreme anger.

Bond

(BAHND) *noun*

A bond is a close connection or friendship.

❓ Do best friends have a bond?

❗ Yes. Best friends have a very special bond!

Hilarious

(huh - **LAYR** - ee - uhs) *adjective*

Something that is hilarious is very funny.

? What do you call a hilarious rabbit?

! A funny bunny!

FTTTTPPPPTT!

Jewel

(JOOL) *noun*

A jewel is a valuable stone, such as a diamond or ruby.

? What kind of rock do you find on someone's finger?

! A jewel!

Clever

(**KLEV** - ur) *adjective*

It's 66!

Correct! You are very clever!

27 + 39 = ?

Someone who is clever is smart, has a bright, quick mind and can easily understand things.

? How is a clever person like a light bulb?

! Both are bright!

Rainbow

(**RAYN** – boh) *noun*

A **rainbow** is an arch of colors
that you can see in the sky
during or after the rain.

? When won't you see a rainbow:
when it's raining, or when it's nighttime?

! You can't see rainbows at night!

Sniffle

(**SNIF** – uhl) *verb*

When you sniffle, you breathe noisily through your nose, often because you have a cold or are crying.

sniffle

sniffle

? Why did the refrigerator sniffle?

! It had a cold!

Champion

(CHAM – pee – uhn) noun

A **champion** is the winner
of a competition.

? Is the dog that comes in last place
at the show a champion?

! No. The dog that comes in first

Accident

(**AK** – si – duhnt) *noun*

An accident is when something unpleasant happens that you did not plan or expect.

? If you fall and hurt yourself, is that an accident?

! Yes. You would not plan or expect to fall.

Squander

(**SKWAHN** – dur) *verb*

To squander something is to waste it. You can squander money or time.

? What can you squander that you will never get back?

! Time!

Occupation

(ahk - yuh - **PAY** - shuhn) *noun*

I'm a baker.

Your occupation is your job.

? Which is an occupation: being a fire fighter, or riding a bike?

! Being a fire fighter is a great occupation.

Awful

(**AW** – fuhl) *adjective*

Awful is another word for terrible, horrible or unpleasant.

What an awful accident!

? What time is it when there's an awful car accident?

! Time to get a new car!

Deliver

(duh – **LIV** – ur) *verb*

To deliver something means to send or bring something to a particular person or place.

? If someone delivers a pizza to you, do you have to go pick it up?

! No. If they deliver it, they bring it to you.

Generous

(**JEN** – ur – uhs) *adjective*

A **generous** person gives more than is expected.

? What should you always say to someone who is generous?

! Thank you very much!

Serious

(**SEER** – ee – uhs) *adjective*

Something that is serious
is very important. Someone
who is serious is not silly
or playful.

? If you are serious about something,
are you kidding around?

! No. When you are serious, you
don't joke.

Sensible

(**SEN** – suh – buhl) *adjective*

If you are sensible, you think about your actions. You don't do silly or dangerous things.

Be sensible. Come down!

? Is wearing a helmet when you ride your bike sensible?

! Yes. Always wear a helmet when you ride your bike!

Bargain

(**BAR** – guhn) *noun*

Sale

A bargain is something that you buy for less than its usual price.

? If you buy a sweater at half price, is that a bargain?

! Yes. Buying something at half price is a bargain.

Dangle
(**DANG** – guhl) *verb*

To dangle **means to hang and swing freely.**

? How is an apple like a monkey?

! Both can dangle from a tree!

Memory

(**MEM** – uh – ree) *noun*

Mom's birthday is Wednesday

I live on Maple Street

2 x 2 = 4

Your memory is your power to remember things.

❓ If your memory is good, do you forget your lunch a lot?

❗ No. If you have good memory, you remember things.

Melody

(**MEL** – uh – dee) *noun*

A melody is a song or tune.

? Which would make a melody: a guitar, or a fire engine?

! A guitar can make a melody, a fire engine makes noise!

Convince

(kuhn – **VINS**) *verb*

When you convince someone of something, you make the person believe you or do what you ask.

? If you convince someone to carry your books, what do they do?

! They happily carry your books!

Translate

(**TRANZ** – layt) *verb*

To translate means to change the words of one language into another language.

Parlez-vous francais?

I'll translate.

Do you speak French?

?

? How do you translate "friend" into Spanish?

! Amigo!

Shrivel

(**SHRIV** – uhl) *verb*

To shrivel is to shrink, dry up or wrinkle from heat or sunlight.

? When a grape dries up and shrivels, what do you get?

! A raisin.

Flame

(**FLAYM**) noun

A flame is a small part of a fire. You can see a flame on a candle.

? Where might you see a flame: in a refrigerator, or in a campfire?

! You would see flames in a campfire.

Charm

(CHAHRM) *noun*

If someone has charm, they behave in a pleasant and nice way.

? What do you call a place where animals are polite and pleasant?

! The charm farm!

Hush

(HUHSH) *noun*

A hush just fell over the chickens!

When there is a hush, it is suddenly quiet.

? What can you tell people if you want them to be quiet?

! Hush, please!

Ripple
(**RIP** - uhl) *noun*

A ripple is a very small wave
on the surface of water.

? Which can cause a ripple:
a rock, wind or a frog?

! All three can cause a ripple.

Vast

(**VAST**) *adjective*

The ocean is so vast and my boat is so small!

A space that is vast is very big and open.

❓ Which would you say is vast: outer space, or your bedroom?

❗ Outer space is vast and endless.

Companion

(kuhm - **PAN** - yuhn) *noun*

A companion is a friend you spend time with.

? What does a pig call his companion?

! A "pen" pal!

Cosmic

(**KAHZ** – mik) *adjective*

It's a cosmic lightshow!

Something cosmic comes from, or belongs to, outer space.

? **Which fish is the most cosmic?**

! A "star" fish!

Original

(uh – **RIJ** – uh – nuhl) *noun, adjective*

An **original** is the first of something. **Original** can also describe something new or unusual.

❓ Is an original comic book the first one of the series?

❗ Yes. The first one is the original. Keep it safe. It might be valuable someday!

Nostril
(NAHS - truhl) *noun*

A **nostril** is one of the two holes at the end of a nose. Your nostrils help you breathe and smell.

❓ How are bumble bees like goldfish?

❗ They don't have nostrils!

Argue

(**AR** – gyoo) *verb*

When you argue, you disagree
with someone. You use words
to strongly share your point
of view.

? You and your sister argue about who will wash the dishes.
Does this mean you agree to do them together?

! No. When you argue, you disagree.

Rumple

(**RUHM** – puhl) *verb*

To rumple is to wrinkle or crease.

? Why doesn't an elephant ever rumple his suit?

! It already has plenty of wrinkles!

Scuttle

(**SKUHT** – uhl) *verb*

When you scuttle, you
run with short, quick steps.

? Crabs scuttle across the beach.
Are they swimming, or running?

! Crabs that scuttle are running.

Blunder

(**BLUHN** - dur) *noun, verb*

A blunder is a careless mistake. To blunder is to make a careless mistake.

What a blunder!

? What should you do if you blunder?

! Try, try again!

Bunch

(BUHNCH) *noun*

A bunch is a group of people or things, such as a bunch of flowers.

? How are grapes like bananas?

! They are both sold in a bunch.

Notice

(NOH – tis) *verb*

To notice means to see
something, or become
aware of it.

**Did you notice
my new hairdo?**

? What did one snail say to the other?

! I notice you moved!

Glimpse

(**GLIMPS**) *verb, noun*

To glimpse means to look at something very quickly. A glimpse is a quick look.

? If you catch a glimpse of a bird, are you looking at it for a long time?

! No. You are taking a quick peek.

Request

(ri - **KWEST**) *verb*

May I request a new bike?

When you request something, you ask for it politely.

? **What can you always request from your best friend?**

! **A smile!**

Diamond

(**DIE** - muhnd) *noun*

A **diamond** is a hard, clear, precious stone. A **diamond** is also a shape.

? How is a jewelry store like a deck of cards?

! Both have diamonds.

Construct

(kuhn – **STRUHKT**) *verb*

To construct something is to build it.

? What do beavers construct?

! Dams.

Optimistic

(ahp - tuh - **MIS** - tik) *adjective*

If you are optimistic, you are hopeful that things will turn out well.

? Why was the boy who liked eggs optimistic about getting an A+?

! He always looked on the "sunny side" of things!

Ignore
(ig - **NOR**) verb

When you ignore something or someone, you don't pay any attention to it.

? Should you ignore your teacher?

! No. You should pay close attention in class!

Capture

(**KAP** - chur) *verb*

I captured a frog!

When you capture someone or something, you catch them.

? What should you do if you capture a frog?

! Treat it kindly, then let it go.

Spoil
(SPOIL) *verb*

Oh no! I spoiled the cake!

To spoil something is to ruin or wreck it.

? How could you spoil a surprise?

! By telling someone about it before it happens!

Hike

(HIEK) *noun, verb*

A hike is a long walk. To hike is to go on a long walk, often in nature.

? What did the puppy say after a long hike?

! I'm dog-tired!

Donate

(**DOH** – nayt) *verb*

When you donate something, you give it away to help others.

I want to donate my toys!

? **If you donate clothes, do you give them away for free?**

! Yes. It's good to donate things to those who need them!

Treatment

(**TREET** – muhnt) *noun*

Treatment **is the care, help or medicine that one person gives another.**

? Where does a sick pony go for treatment?

! A "horse-pital"!

Permission

(pur - **MISH** - uhn) *noun*

95

May I have permission to go to the bathroom?

If you give someone permission to do something, you say it is okay for them to do it.

? What does a gorilla need permission to do?

! Nothing. Gorillas do whatever they want!

Author

(**AW** - thur) *noun*

An author is the writer of a
book, play, poem or article.

❓ If a hog becomes an author, how
does he write his book?

❗ With a "pig-pen"!

Waver

(**WAY** - vur) *verb*

To waver about something is to be uncertain about it.

❓ What is the favorite answer of someone who likes to waver?

❗ Yes—and no!

Gentle

(**JEN** – tuhl) *adjective*

Someone gentle is kind and sensitive.

❓ Why was the duck being gentle with her eggs?

❗ She didn't want to "quack" them!

Ache

(**AYK**) *noun*

My tummy aches!

An ache is a strong, steady pain.

? If someone lies about their ache, what do they have?

! A fake ache!

Purchase

(**PUR** – chuhs) *verb, noun*

I'd like to purchase this, please!

To purchase something means to buy it. A purchase is also the thing you have bought.

? Why did the lion purchase a lamp?

! He wanted to light up his "den".

Praise

(PRAYZ) *verb*

Way to go!

When you praise someone, you tell the person that they have done a good job.

Report Card
A
A
A
A

? Why did the student praise the teachers?

! Because she had a lot of class!

Debris

(duh - **BREE**) *noun*

Debris is the scattered pieces of something that has been broken up and destroyed.

? Could a strong storm leave branches and other debris in your yard?

! Yes. Debris can be made up of broken branches and limbs.

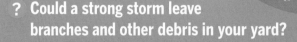

Statue

(**STACH** – oo) *noun*

A statue is a large model of a person or animal made of wood, stone, metal or other things.

? What did the silly policeman say to the statue?

! Freeze! Don't move!

Rapid

(**RAP** - id) *adjective*

Rapid **means very quick or fast.**

? **If you are on a rapid train, will you get where you are going quickly?**

! Yes—a rapid train moves very fast!

Brilliant

(**BRIL** – yuhnt) *adjective*

Something that is brilliant shines very brightly.

? How is a diamond like the sun?

! Both can be brilliant!

Holler

(**HAHL** - ur) *verb*

To holler means to yell.

? Why did the mother bird holler at the baby bird?

! She didn't want to hear a peep out of him!

Index